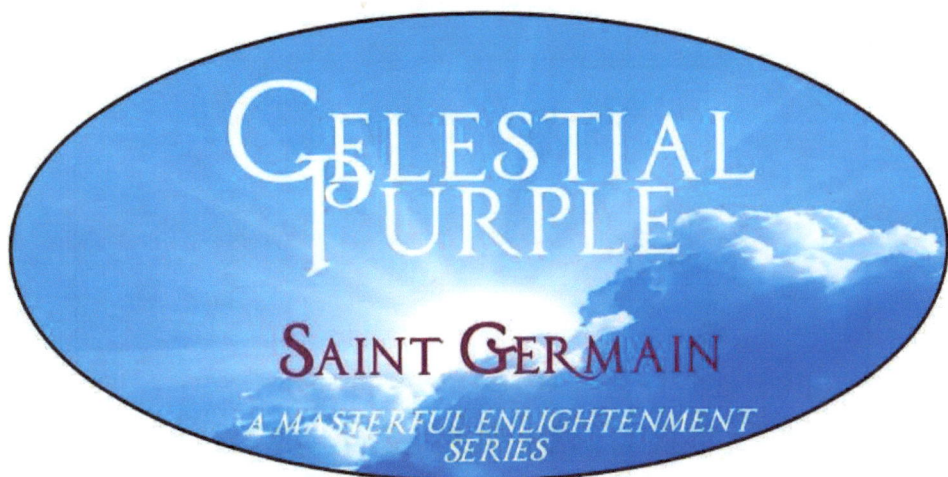

CELESTIAL PURPLE

SAINT GERMAIN

A MASTERFUL ENLIGHTENMENT SERIES

Volume 1

DUALITY

IN

PERSPECTIVE

PART I

*SPIRIT SOURCED * HUMAN MADE*

AI FREE

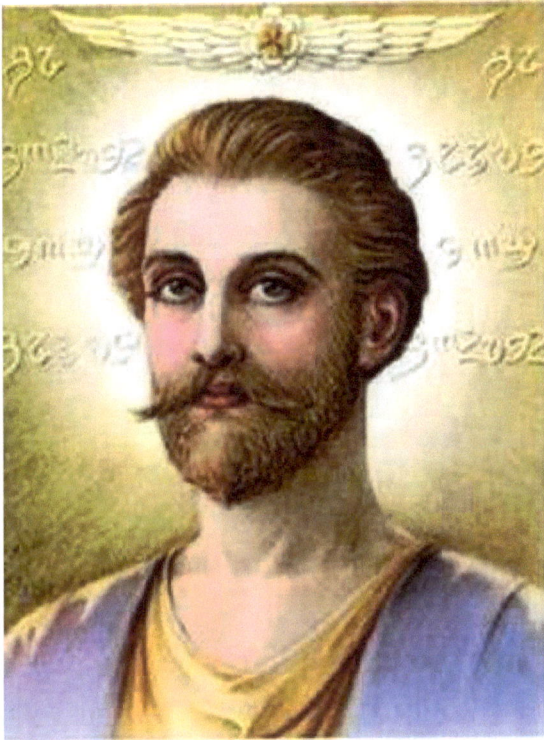

Saint Germain

Portrait Charles Sindelar

Books by This Author

⍦ ⍦

THE SAINT GERMAIN CHRONICLES COLLECTION
A Journey Into Practical Spirituality

VICTORY FOR THE SOUL
Relationships That Work

RISING ABOVE
A Journey To Higher Dimensions

TRUE COMPASSION
Merging Love Into Oneness

TRUST AND BETRAYAL

DUALITY
In Perspective

GORDON CORWIN II aka LAH RAHN ANANDA   Amazon   www.SaintGermainchronicles.com

⦾VERIVEW

For all Humanity, Duality continues to be an ongoing mysterious enigma, an ever-present impactive band of Earth energy that affects all Mankind and living things.

This enlightening Saint Germain discourse describes the Divine construction of Duality and sharply contrasting energies. Your perception and relationship to Duality is shown to be of gigantic importance, directly impacting the quality of your every-day Human life-stream.

Learn how these opposite yet interconnected energy forces can become accepted or experienced as confrontational, both in tandem with the interplay of Free-will choice. Your Man-made perceptions, distinct from Raw Duality, are bluntly exposed, … as filled with their habitual judgments, opinions, and common Ego-based illusions that bear cost and burden.

A Healing process is offered to the aware and receptive, guiding Ones in the wise use of Free-will choice, … actions targeted to shift *perceived burdens* of Duality as an enemy into a grounded *reality of* 'what is' and consequently into a *'friend'*. Accept this invitation to enjoy the fruits of this transformation process. Empower yourself by anchoring your perceptions of Duality into alignment, Truth, and Freedom along your path of a quality and an extraordinary lifetime.

With Love and Blessings to All,

LAH RAHN ANANDA

DUALITY
IN
PERSPECTIVE

Through Lah Rahn Ananda 03-11-2023

Many are wondering, at this point in Human consciousness evolvement, about that unique band of energy named **DUALITY** that surrounds your Earth World, a condition of Creation imposed upon living things and Beings.

Perplexing as this reality indeed can be, Humans are attempting, often in vain or simply in ignorance, to reconcile the positive and negative forces that seem, at times, to invade your everyday lives, ... and further, to understand why Yin-Yang energies can, ... if allowed by *your perception*, ... hold you in their grip, ... as Duality's *opposite but interconnected forces* have their way with you.

Be aware, as **We begin, that the energy of Duality** is one of several characteristic energy phenomena that wrap around Planet Earth and engage with Humanity. As with other energies that you Humans are obliged to navigate while enrolled in the Earth School, your *perception of and attitude toward Duality* will greatly affect the overall quality of your Human experience, … the quality of your life.

B y now, you may have noticed that Free-will choice is a close relative of Duality, if not its ever-present spouse. We shall further explore this aspect -- be patient.

When you navigate the energies of Duality as a Human, Ego's perception will often invite you to become

entangled, …   using
free-will choice

Can you see   where
We are going?   Buckle
up your seat   belts, My
Friends. Here   comes the
enigma for All   Humanity
at this point, … the **age-old trap of**

perceiving as 'good or bad' an Earthly energy field about which mankind is at effect and yet has no control. This would be the Domain of pure Duality, before Mankind superimposes certain convoluted perceptions into the mix.

As you ponder this a bit, hold your Ego at bay, ... to attune your resonation and vibration with this Truth. Then, you will be aligned to proceed with intaking that of   which   I AM about to speak.

Alright!

L et Me shed some Light upon this enigma. As Creation was having its way and as Earth was being prepared for Human inhabitation, it was meant that the gift of Free-will for Earthlings need be tied to the Duality energy. And so it was. Duality was introduced **and** remains so, ... injected into Earth's Energy Aura.

A mystical combination *of Free-will choice, consequences of Ego behaviors, and Karmic accountability* are all woven together as Duality takes impact upon Human Life-streams.

You then, as a Human, have inherited with your incarnation, a unique interconnected arrangement of energies in this context, ... Free-will, Duality, and Karma, all Divinely linked together as part of the *Earth-school platform*, as digitally obsessed Humans might phrase it. (Master – chuckles mmmm)

By now you may have noted the interconnections I refer to? And yes, have you noted, in full awareness, that this Duality Energy is *unavoidably pervasive in Human life* upon Earth, reaching right down into the knubs of your own momentary and daily choices and behaviors. Yes?

In this particular context as We begin, I shall allow *the mere understanding* of a phenomenon to suffice as a requisite to further needed awareness of *Knowing and ultimately Being*. Let *Being* be a conversation at rest for another day.

Obvious and undeniable examples of Duality in action are couched in well-known contrasts of winter - summer, yes - no, male - female, day - night,   expanding - contracting, asleep - awake, order vs. chaos, ... along with others I shall later site for you.

Earthly Duality is one of Earth's *specific energy fields* surrounding its plane, ... an energy that provides needed perspectives of extreme opposites, ... present and undeniable, ... affecting Human life-streams as one part of the *full and entire* massive energy field that surrounds your Mother Earth.

Duality presents these contrasting opposites, …extremes, which if embraced, provide valuable openings for Human healing and evolution of consciousness wrapped in your life-lessons. This scenario may then, if your Ego will surrender and allow entry into the broader picture of your life-stream, open possibilities for wise and insightful life-choices lain upon your table.

However, when Ego resists, We Above see denial and resistance surfacing as the most common lower Dimensional response to Duality. This lack of open-minded awareness and receptivity blunts

The function of Duality's band of energy, … one of many God-created Blessings surrounding your Planet, … serves to impose upon Humanity a celestially unique Earthly phenomenon/reality (not necessarily a Universal energy reality) that presents and demonstrates contrast, opening the door for higher *Human awareness leading to choices of Perspective, … or not.*

delicious opportunities for making wise choices and can thereby result in life-long struggles. With eyes open wide, this *Ego behavior is apparent* in countless aspects of Human behavior, around your Earth World. Can you observe this?

Like it or not, Duality is here to stay for you to
navigate as part of the *Human Condition.*
Tempting as it may be to identify yourself as it's
victim, you will eventually awaken to this Truth.

**In essence, you have inherited this unique
band of Duality energy as an *unnegotiable*
condition of your Human incarnation.**

ल्ल ल्ल

When, as a next step forward, you *surrender to
include this perspective that I now offer to you as
part of the 'what is'* … you truly gift yourself with
an empowering range of free-will choices to
embrace, … in favor of otherwise inviting more
struggling and locking yourself out of
synchronicities to come.

Surrendered to 'what is', You are then standing
at the *threshold of the open door of wise free-will
choice.* You have, of course, an alternative, … to
struggle in rejection, with Ego as your guide. We
sadly observe the latter to be *Humanity's default
behavior* in this context.

The sharply pointed opposite of resistance to
these Truths is a choice to *awaken from the victim
mentality* and to pursue your upward path of
conscious evolution … moving upward upon the
rungs of the Spiritual Ladder, … in alignment with
Spirit's teachings and your consequent potential
levels of higher vibration.

So, what will it be?

A lright! So here you stand. Duality is
unrelentingly staring you in the face, day
by day, night by night. And either
consciously or unwittingly, you often struggle,
kick, and scream, not fully knowing how to
navigate this energy field. Yes? Or Yes?

Strangely and ironically enough, this can become
a perplexing phenomenon to grasp, pervasive as it
is in your lives, and yet while *simultaneously
presenting Blessings.*

Here lies another opportunity for broadening your
perspectives, in this case of encountering opposites,
as stark contrasts you may choose to observe, *…
and if you are wise …, without judgment!*

Contained inside of the full perspective that Duality brings to the 'Earth-school, is a multitude of different shades and varying grey areas. And yes, let us bypass the argument that would pull you off track. We shall stick to the heart of the matter.

For this purpose, let Us now look in greater depth at the contrasting opposites that Duality offers up for your awareness and launch a beginning edification of this phenomenon.

In the inception, certain fundamental roots of Duality appear for Humans at infancy and early ages, underscoring this segment of your development ... and later on, lighting the way for wise, ...or not, ... free-will choices, bearing Duality in mind. For 5th Dimensional Ones and beyond, *these choices* reflect an embrace of 'what is' and become pleasantly automatic, as life goes on with exponentially greater ease and grace, ... as wise choices allow One Rises Above Into Higher Dimensions.

To further clarify and illustrate my point about opposites, yes, I say again, *shades of grey* are present in the mix. Put your Ego aside and intake the *Wisdom of perspective* I bring. Get the point, without *inner arguments* about the exceptions and the shades of grey that are etched in your consciousness. Get the point!

D

uality, at it's polar extremes, presents contrasts of opposites, such as:

Positive and negative,

Open and closed,

Light and dark,

Up and down,

Pro and con,

Yes and no,

Pregnant or not pregnant, (Master chuckles hmmmm)

Included and excluded,

Expanding and contracting,

Constructive – Destructive,

Physically alive and physically dead

Left and right,

… as examples meant to illustrate the 'what is' Duality observed with a resulting lack of judgment .

I interject for you an accurate variation, akin to 'good and bad', penned by one of your talented script writers and film makers, … who states simply *'There is no right or wrong, there is only what is and what is not'.*

Ponder this for a moment.

Now …… notice here, how Mankind's Ego with judgments slyly edging their way into the game, resulting in MAN-MADE realities, … *believed* to be fundamentally coupled to the field of Duality, … and THEN LABELED as Duality, when actually these beliefs and resulting behaviors are merely products of Man's own judgmental doing!

The root misconception of Duality is now exposed, Chaps and Lassies!

I speak of the labeling of various aspects of Duality as   Good and Bad.

> **Note well, … these labels grip multitudes standing on the slippery slope of your 3rd Dimensional consciousness platform, … where *Full Permission is given for judgment* … Fully endorsed by societal agreement for such behavior!**

Variations of 'good and/or bad' Human 3rd Dimensional judgments may include:

Winner or loser!

Better or worse,

Smart and dumb, Brilliant or idiot,

Strong or weak,

Success or Failure,

Pretty or ugly, (remember beauty is in the eye of the beholder), etc. etc.

What are your conclusions about these extremes? With which societal group do you align? What shall be your future *practice about judging and labeling* as you go through your life! What will be your Free-will *choices when Duality calls at your door*, when it presents itself into your life- stream?

You may note that certain Ones navigating their lives, … often sourced at a deep Karmic level, … *choose to allow judgmental practices rooted deep their consciousnesses.* Consequently, exagerated practices of judgment *hold\and exude a magnified negative energy field of darkness*. This can pervade thinking patterns that also bleed into these Auras, … felt and sometimes visible by other Humans. **This pattern can be healed** with **diligence and Love,** reintroducing Light that once was. Optimistically note My upcoming pages about **Transmuting Judgment** and the 4 Step Process I endorse! Sadly though, if allowed to progress, an ultimately challenging condition can morph into 'a period of Spiritual desolation and depression in which a sense of consolation is removed', … as would be described by your Earthly sources.

Your acceptance of the Truths I speak can bring you *into alignment, at your choice,* …at various levels of awareness, … moment by moment. Read on and note *that these choices can become a Blessing or a Burden.*

The Dual range choice is one of <u>Full Acceptance,</u> or being at odds with Duality, judging the inevitable in *ways that make it your enemy*, your adversary, your burden, your annoyance, etc. etc.

So here is the point.

<u>Judging an Earthly Phenomenon in a negative context, places the burden upon you.</u> *And yet the masses of Humanity have yet to realize this fact.* The cost is great! Freedom and happiness have been placed at risk. They are at stake! **Along with limiting your synchronicities!**

Your freedom is restricted, as you may twist and squirm at the effect of Duality that enters your livestream.

Realigning your Perception of Duality, *moment by moment*, *will relieve your burdens and deliver an amazing and ongoing new senses of Freedom* … if you so choose. It is called *harmony*, Folks! This healing process takes extreme awareness, discipline, and perseverance. Moment by moment, until new behavior becomes automatic, as a fine habit!

ॐ ॐ

ॐ

Being

Living

Knowing

Intake

Inquiry

The Process

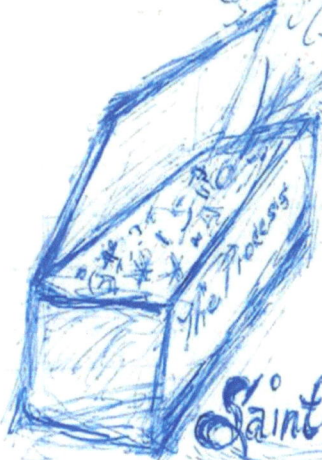

Saint Germain's Tool Box

Lali Kahn 2023

H
ere now, let Me bring a bit of ease and grace to your process.

Like many other tools in My *Saint Germain Spiritual Toolbox of Being*, there be one in particular existentially *One's regard reaction Duality.* that influences *and toward* Do you know what this is?

That would be your **automatic behavior** *to refrain from JUDGMENT* ,… as blatantly different aspects of Duality show up in your life-stream!

Mastering this ability and fully placing this Divine behavior into your consciousness, … moment by moment, … will serve to invite Peace, Harmony and Love into the very core of your Blessed Being. If you want your 'guarantee', this IS one! (Master chuckles hhhmmm mmm).

Surrendering your Ego resistance to this ancient Human habit of judgment is a tall order for any Human moving through the process of evolvement, I admit. The benefits, however, are far, far, far reaching!

Entry into the 5th Dimension and progressing to live in the Higher 7th and 9th Dimensions, … requires full Mastery of this ability in each of your moments. Can you see the immense importance?

The appearance of Dual *elements* in your life, such as dark and light, yin and yang, positive and negative, constructive and destructive, … as examples, … *can be more fluidly accepted with free-will surrender* … be allowed within your Personal Universe, … when you simply learn to accept Duality as a part of 'what is'. Accept 'what is' and let it BE. And, with the important codicil that this 'letting it BE' is **willingly done …** ABSENT, of course, *your endorsement of or wish to prolong difficult times that Duality may impose.* (Master chuckles about the irony here , addictions to pain … hmmmmm).

Ignoring this codicil is an opening to trigger *victim mentality* that can feed upon negativity. This also shall be a conversation for another day.

And now, … to the healing!

The below Diagram will illustrate a process of healing for you to transcend from a challenging circumstance into Freedom. You would do well to pin this picture on your refrigerator door, Chaps and Lassies!

Embracing Duality

FREEDOM
Alignment
Self-correction
Non-Judgment
Choice
Surrender
Perspective
Awareness and Focus

CIRCUMSTANCE

35

Alright! We have come thus far regarding your **awareness** about <u>resistance of surrendering judgments</u> (a poignant example of transcending <u>the effects</u> of Duality at work, ... (Master chuckles   haa mmmm).

Now comes the slippery slope.

Typical Human behavior seems to draw a sharp line at this point. When Duality stares you in the face, you have, no doubt, encountered difficult choices. That is to say, when these conditions appear to grip your circumstances, and you are *<mark>yet to be</mark>* in the consciousness of 'what is', <u>intense feelings can invade your Being.</u> These can easily lead you down the *slippery slope of Judgment*, ... and the *<u>temptation to label a circumstance as 'Good or Bad'. Nota Bene!   Labeling is under your control, Folks!</u>*

As I spoke unto all Humanity as Shakespeare over 200 Earth years now past, ... *"there is no good or bad, it is simply your thinking that makes it so".*

Does this ring a bell?
Ponder this a moment before you read on.

Widely accepted <u>man-made beliefs</u> are often fabricated using *good and bad* as their center core. *This pattern engulfs your entire Earthly civilization! The practice crosses all boundaries including race, age, gender, culture, and even your religions.* This may shock some of you.

We observe from Above that with Human Judgments in full swing, you yourselves, along with your various World societies, typically and reactively impose these Man-made fabrications, … willy-nilly, … tenderly caressed, <u>locked within your individual and collective belief systems, as Truth.</u>

By using *habitual labeling*, you All have compounded the 'What is' <u>with your Judgments of 'What is'</u> … in this case as 'good or bad', for example. <u>You compound the impact of Duality!</u>

Such behavior superimposes the energy of your Human judgments *on top of, and often contra to, an Earth energy over which you have no control!*

Such behavior *traps your vibration* in the lower parts of the 3rd Dimension, a consciousness that will surround you until you allow a healing of your ways. Sad but True. Once again, the choice is yours.

<u>What a pickle you put yourself into!</u>

Can you see how your Ego fails to serve as your Bona-fide guide, but *purports to engage you in a struggle of changing the 'what is'?*

O H MY! Countless other internal and external conflicts that lurk in a Human life-stream are *also centered around this habitual, incessant behavior of Judgment!* Can you not see this as plain as day in your own life?

Can you also see that your full surrender and non-judgmental behavior will *pull you off of this slippery slope*, … and place your feet upon tera firma, … firm ground upon which to stand in some balance, … with space for synchronicity to enter your life, … to align with The Divine, and the 'what is', … and to invite peace, harmony and Love that you dream about?

In delightful surrender with a broader perspective in place, Humans are equipped with *an aware spectrum of* free-will choices, … rather than knee-jerk resistance. Wise choices may then follow a healled Perception and have their effects. Re-view the previous Embracing Duality diagram to re-enforce your process, Dear Ones!

❧ ❧

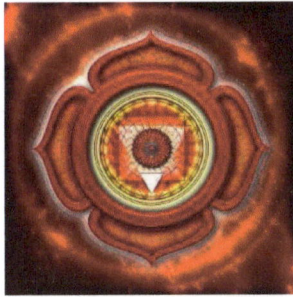

M y intention is to awaken and enlighten you along with All Humanity.

Once again, with this healing, your aware Free-will choices have come into play. All encompassing. Be assured, your wise choices shall pay immense Spiritual dividends. Be also well assured, ... they shall lead you into higher Dimensions of Vibration, ... further into an Extra-ordinary life that is worth living, ... a life filled with Love, Soul satisfaction, peace, and Well-being.

Your daily awareness of holding Duality in non-judgement will initiate *a focus upon the self-correction* to make this so. This is a gift from you to you.

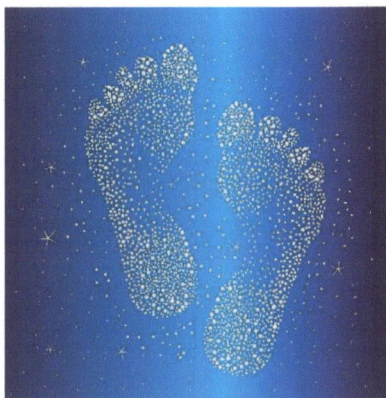

Conquering judgments as I describe is a mammoth Human achievement in Ego Mastery, Good Friends! It paves the way into the 5th Dimension that you all are talking about now, 2023 Earth year. Note well also, that without this Mastery, the 3rd Dimension shall remain your home! Evolvement serves no free lunch in this respect!

Mastery of -non-judgment is akin to the all-inclusive process that applies to *befriending our own EGO*, Folks. This Ego-neutralizing theme song I have sung countless times. It is abundantly clear throughout My many transmissions and books over the past 25 years now through your Lah Rahn Ananda, ... a Blessed Earth-Partner of the Spirit Realm, a Being whom I now source and shall embrace forever.

45

I suggest *you Bless yourself* by acquiring these works and intake the vast well-spring of Wisdom I have aggregated as My Blessing to Humanity. If not in this lifetime, perhaps in future incarnations you will discover these treasures, … when you choose to awaken more fully, … and yes, Carpe Diem! In this book, as in all of My books, I fully support you with the finest Light of Spirit to harken and apply the Wisdom I bring, stepping forward into *your new skin of all you can Be, the finest version of Being Human.*   *Honor your Highest-self and your Soul to BE Divinely Blessed by internalizing the various aspects of Higher Spiritual Being,… presented unto you and All Humanity in My other books:*

∽ **All Amazon available** ⤍

Trust and Betrayal,
A Challenge of Choice

Victory For The Soul,
Relationships That Work

Rising Above,
A Journey Into Higher Dimensions

True Compassion
Merging Love into Oneness

The Saint Germain Chronicles Collection,
A Journey Into Practical Spirituality

*B*e Blessed, My Dearest Ones, Be wise, and bathe yourself in the beauty and Love that being Human can offer you while the door is open!

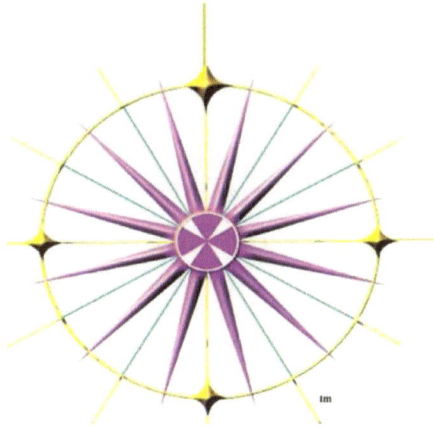

Saint Germain

and Lah Rahn aka Gordon Corwin II Ananda

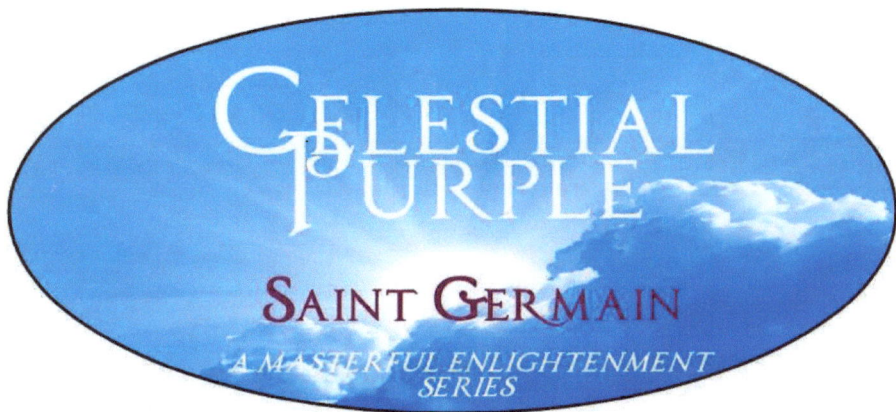

CELESTIAL PURPLE

SAINT GERMAIN

A MASTERFUL ENLIGHTENMENT SERIES

Volume 1

DUALITY

EXCHANGING YOUR JUDGMENTS FOR OBSERVATIONS

PART II

Saint Germain

SPIRIT SOURCED * HUMAN MADE

AI FREE

With deeper insights into the devastating impact of judgment-making in your life, you will eventually realize the immense triggering impact of your judgments upon your perceptions of DUALITY. As you will discover at some point, there is an excessive cost to making judgments that later feed opinions and source beliefs versus simply observing and seeking Truth. The costs and burdens of making naked judgments throughout your days and nights are the behaviors I shall address as the focus of this dissertation today.

We Ascended Above observe common Human judgment patterns to be centered around judgments of: 'I'm right and you are wrong', 'better than and less than', 'good or bad', etc.

Such often denigrating judgments can conveniently demonstrate One's defense against low self-esteem and insecurity as well as sheer arrogance. Such Ego indulgent behaviors, later becoming entrenched as beliefs, are widely **Humans who carry forth an 'I'm right' attitude**.

==As We together begin==, open your Heart-space to the Truth about your learned *patterns of judgment*, likely <u>habitual by now</u>, because Humans upon your Earth are living predominantly within a *Third Dimensional (3-D) society construct, <u>where Ego commonly reigns supreme</u>.*

Asking you to rescind your judgment habits and behaviors, many endorsed by your societies *and* leaders, is indeed a tall order as I have spoken in Part I of this discourse.

In fact, this non-judgment transmutation of consciousness is ironically 'judged' and labeled by some as a Super-Human request! (Master chuckles hmmmm).   At the same time, I AM confident that you who seek awareness leading to Higher Dimensions of consciousness, above the 3rd Dimension, will be *heartfully receptive to the **Wisdom and Healing Process I now bring forth upon the following pages.***

<u>**Held tightly in the clutches of Third Dimensional consciousness customs**</u>, … confusingly intermixed and entwined with DUALITY upon Earth, … You have *unwittingly* been given permission by the collective World society to JUDGE. For the masses of Humanity, … and yes, there are evolved exceptions, … **judging is at the very core of Human EGO behavior**.

Recognizing this Truth and being open to transcending this enormously burdening habit of behavior, … you may now *choose* to be drawn into an **entirely ...**

New Freedom of Being

through transcending your judgments, … in every instant!

I speak here of developing for yourself an automatic, new habit and discipline about the way in which you hold your influx of events and circumstances ... *incoming instantaneously to your consciousness,* ... **to Be newly suspended in pure observation of 'What Is.'**

I could elucidate and write for eons about this act of surrender on your part, *and yet these vastly empowering new energies that replace judgment will escape your grasp unless you act to diligently apply this discipline in every moment of your life.* Yes, in each instant, as your brain whirls around and senses Earth energies that accost and attract your attention, *seemingly* begging to be judged.

For those of you Humans that would remain *unaware* of the opportunity to transcend your judgments, ... or Ones aware but simply unwilling to make change, ... you are destined to remain confined to the *crib of the Third Dimension*, sad but True ... and held in the 3-D, where your upward evolvement shall remain stymied with resultant further revolutions to follow upon the Karmic wheel. Your Free-will choice.

TRANSCENDING INTO UNCONDITIONAL LOVE

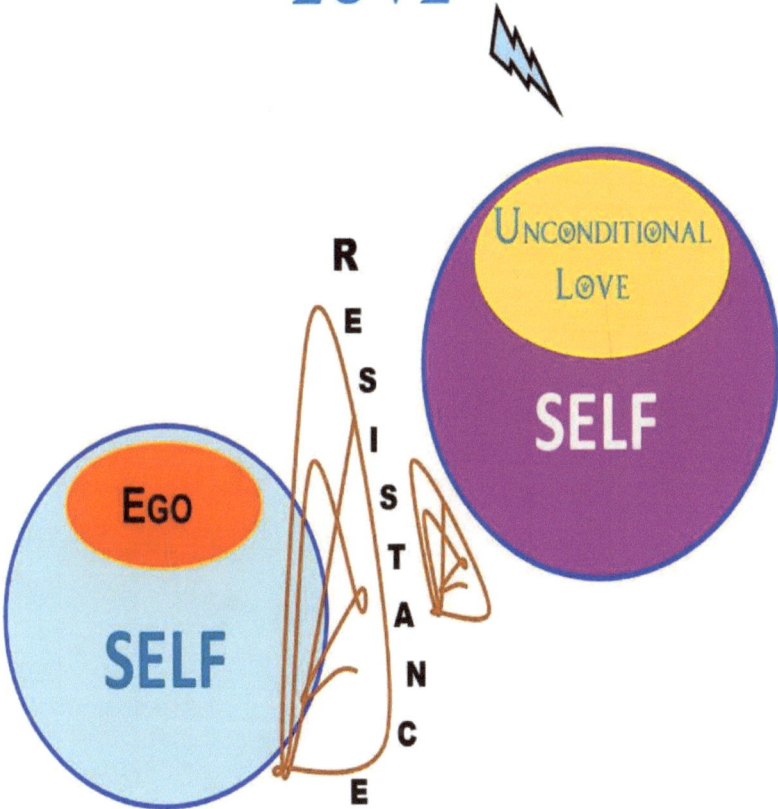

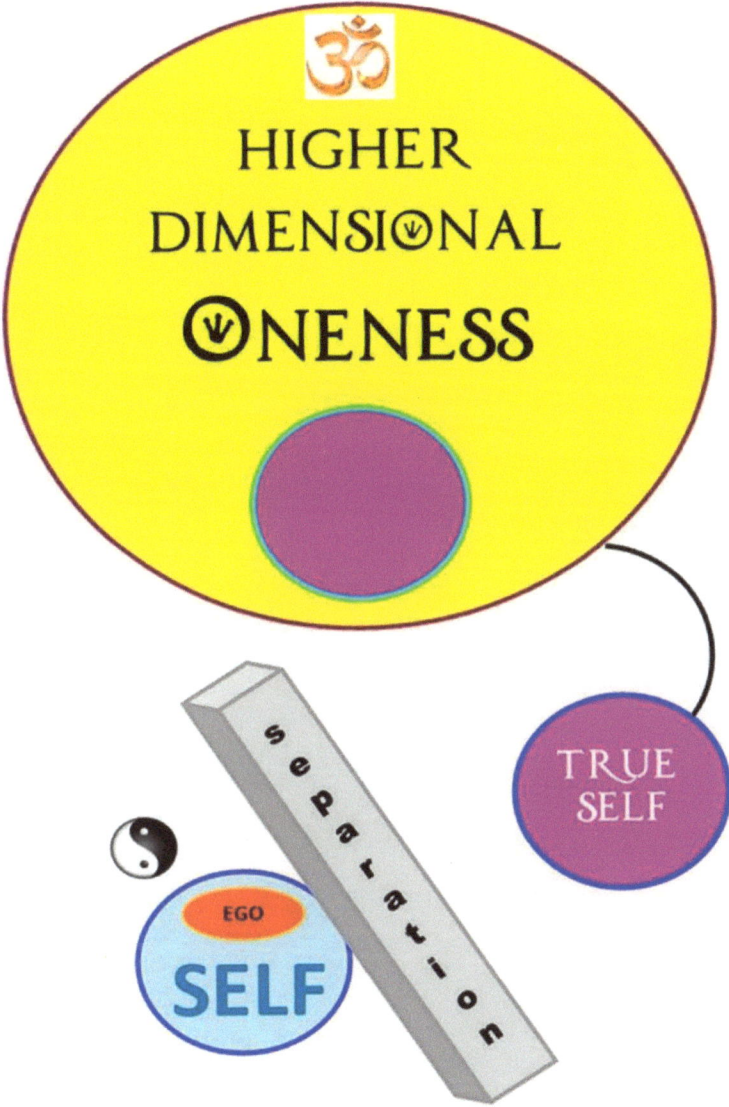

HIGHER DIMENSIONAL ONENESS

TRUE SELF

separation

EGO

SELF

For the wise however, eager to be freed from Duality's ties that can bind, the Discipline of neutral Observation in exchange for Judgment will serve up magnificent rewards, happiness, and Blessings into the resulting natural flow of energies into your Lifestream. *The inflow of Light* is one such energy you will joyfully experience with this Mastery.

 This self-inflicted heavy load of judgment-making upon your shoulders can be lifted and actually eradicated and disbursed by practicing this *new healing discipline* in your thinking patterns… and consequently in healing your belief system.

Here, I AM presenting to you TRUTHS about *judgment behavior healing*. Some will ignore this opportunity for a massive change and pivotal healing in favor of holding on to their status quo judgments and opinions with abounding Ego satisfaction anchored foremost.

And for the open minded who seek attaining higher vibrations of consciousness through their evolvement process, I speak now of re-training yourself in *your personal judgment department* with these 4 steps:

Transmuting Judgments

1. **To** <u>recognize when</u> you are judging.

2. **To** <u>consciously shift your orientation</u> about the circumstance / person **over to** <u>a vibration that access your Higher Spirit-self</u> ... *in real time* ... right in the midst of the very person / circumstance/ event you are judging. Needs your immediate attention to simply observe ... and *without any energy* placed upon judgment. (<u>VICTORY FOR THE SOUL</u> *Relationships that Work*, is one of My latest books, 2022, explaining this process in depth). Gift yourself!

You must want to do this! (If your *Ego payoff is greater* than your commitment to evolve and Be Free, you will merely re-confirm your judgment habit pattern ... and re-main stuck in the mud. Many Third Dimensional behaviors carry a high price and bear a cost of absent happiness. (Let this be not your choice).

3. <u>With full awareness, **To** consciously choose to replace your judgment,</u> *at this instant*, with the new *habit* of invoking your heart energy of True Compassion for the person / situation / circumstance, ... OR, in the alternative, if not your choice as merit-worthy, as I have earlier   described, simply let your observation *rest as a neutral discernment. Still non-judged! Capisce?*

4. To <u>Consciously hold this higher vibrational reoriented energy in place ...</u> surrendering to 'What Is' about the circumstance or the person ... and more importantly... to *your new action to use this newly committed* <u>*PROCESS of non-judgment*</u> *from this moment forward forever.*

Whilst you may newly embrace such a change in your process, beware that this *energy* is created from your heart space... and will remain so as long as you *hold this heart vibration intact.*

 Having cemented this re-training pattern into your habit patterns of thinking, your consciousness ... and into your new Way of Being, ... you shall emerge Victorious.

And , ... with a bonus *Blessing of a new way of relating to 'What Is'*, You are then set free from the Judgment Burden and the cost it bears.

A pause here, as I offer some refinement.

I Lovingly encourage you to be Soulfully aware of a crucial pit-fall when you reach to *fully embrace* DUALITY and /or other energies as well. Ones learning to *fully EMBRACE* are often temped to sell themselves short by compromising upon a minimal commitment, ... that would be *to merely TOLERATE the CHANGE*. In this mode, you acquiesce. You have strayed off of the path and miss the target!

Using the Spiritual tools in your Saint Germain toolbox of Wisdom (see previous Diagram) will greatly accelerate the installation of this new practice ... **exchanging judgment for Compassion.** Think of it as installing a new APP (as you would) say) into your consciousness, (Master chuckles heartily .. hmmmm hmmm. "I have more downloads © available' haahh hmmm)

If you are wise, you will gratefully wrap your heart and hands around this process and use these tools ongoingly, … and in this case, deliver a magnificent quantum of *Self-love, embracing thyself in this process* along with the practice of **True Compassion.**

This is the litmus test!

The following diagram offers you further perspective on the matter. As you meditate upon this image, start in your Heart-center, aware of your feelings from within, and allow your Ego to be coaxed aside... *to let go of being right*, as expressed by many of your former judgments.

At these wondrous upward points of arrival, *you move toward elevating your consciousness from Knowing to Living,* wrapped in the healing Heart energy of the **5th Dimension of Human consciousness** ... a marvelous place to reside ... for now … as you evolve.

HEALING YOUR JUDGMENTS INTO ONENESS

CREATOR

ONENESS

COMPASSION

LOVE

JUDGMENTS

YOUR LIFE'S CIRCUMSTANCES

Saint Germain 02-2023

75

A miraculous healing takes place during this retraining process, where the compounded Freedoms of non-judgment and Compassion are born anew within your heart and mind, ... underscoring Divinely Blessed energies to be seated into your Here and Now Presence. Together, We have manifested a true *Victory For The Soul*, yours forever.

With Our fondest Blessings,

𝕾𝖆𝖎𝖓𝖙 𝕲𝖊𝖗𝖒𝖆𝖎𝖓
And Lah Rahn Ananda

February 27, 2023

TUNING UP YOUR VIBRATIONS

~ Applied Spirituality from Saint Germain ~

EGO Behavior *compared with*

"My small story is what counts!" Over dramatizes.
Is selfishly focused, ignoring Unity consciousness.

Ego confuses its small story with Reality!
Indulges in *fear-based behavior*, including anger.

Strives to be "important". The BIG shot! Greedy!

"I'm always right" attitude. Arrogant. Believes
Ego's *opinion* is correct! Ignores Human fallibility.
Re-enforces a sagging self-esteem by denial.

My opinion, i.e., "*my* truth", IS *the* Truth!!!
"There are no other possibilities but mine!"

Self-Aggrandizes. *Dominates* selfishly to
over- ride or restrict others' Free-will choices.
Makes untenable excuses. Projects the blame
onto another one/thing. "It's someone else's fault".
Avoids accountability and responsibility.

Complains about *unfulfilled expectations*.
Demands *immediate* satisfaction!
Prefers *complaining* to implementing solutions!
Gets "stuck" on irreconcilable issues

Obsesses about dissatisfactions.

Escalates frustration into anger and hate.
Enjoys being angry; regards as acceptable!
Impatience accelerates into anger.
Believes anger or hate get the best results,

Uses anger to "bully" others, often hiding *fear.*
Promotes conflict and greed. Seeks revenge.
Unable and or unwilling to *recognize emotions.*

Satisfied staying stuck in Egos's versions
of unlearned life's lessons.

Attached to Ego as a prisoner of its own device.

Your Highest-Self Choices

Overcomes EGO's burning indulgence.
Replaced with *aligned self-choices for
highest good.*
Learns, applies, *and* remembers life's lessons.
*Embraces this process with empathy and
overshining fear of* change.
Knows Joy through *humility* and helpfulness.

Seeks Truth, applying the merit of different
perspectives to each moment of every day life.
Replaces denial with reality and self-integrity!

Discerns the *difference* between their
belief system and *Universal/ law / Truth.*

Seeks Mastery of Spirit's teachings of Truth.
See The Saint Germain Chroniclers Collection.
Knows Truth and accepts reality with Joy.
Pacifies an untamed EGO into submission
into its rightful role. Promotes harmony.

Demonstrates patience by shrinking EGO's
stature, now relegated *to take a back seat.*

Seeks out and implements creative
Win-win solutions.
Replaces complaints without squandering energy.
Expresses gratefulness. Sees Blessings!

Utilizes Saint Germain's
healing techniques as presented in His book
'Victory for the Soul, Relationships That Work',
Gordon Corwin II -Lah Rahn Ananda, Amazon.

Recognizes o w n behavior in real-time.
Elevates negative emotions, raising them up into
Neutral or Positive zones.
Is accountable for Own Behaviors.

Fully ENJOYS the Mastery and rewards
of Aligned Actions and Higher Dimensions.
Discovers the Human Condition!
Transcends the Human Illusion!!

Aligns consciousness with Universal /
Divine Law, *freeing their Highest-Self to BE.*

"To Truly Be or not to BE is Your Question". Saint Germain
Through Lah Rahn Ananda 05/2010 Rev. 07/2022

About the Author

Gordon Corwin II, also known as Lah Ran Ananda, translated literally as 'God Light Messenger', is a native Californian, educated at UC Berkeley, followed by service as a Commissioned US Naval Officer, and by extensive careers in the computer and real estate industries.

In 1995, Gordon clearly heard Lord Saint Germain's resounding and mysterious voice from Above, recruiting him to immediately engage with Ascended Spirit and follow his Soul's calling to reactivate his considerable past life Atlantean DNA channeling abilities, and to begin walking his Dharma to serve Humanity!

As an appointed Masters' Representative, Lah Rahn then began delivering Ascended energies through channeling of the Masters' words and visual media, which would now become his changed and conscious life path. In 1998 he founded The Light of the Soul Foundation, a qualified non-profit entity for advanced Spiritual education and Human philanthropy.

Following years of ego-cleansing by the Masters and his upward movement through Higher Dimensions of consciousness, Lah Rahn Ji has, for 25 years now, delivered clear and engaging channelings in public and private Spiritual events along with potent and enlightening mentoring of Chelas in The Light of the Soul Vortex in Southern California.

In 2007 he was highly honored to be chosen by Lord Saint Germain to be the Ascended Masters' instrument and Partner to begin, and later complete, this precise and accurate channeling to Earth of The Saint Germain Chronicles Collection, *A Journey Into Practical Spirituality 2008-2014.* In 2020 Lah Rahn again partnered with Saint Germain to author Victory for The Soul, *Relationships that Work, pub 2022,* and RISING ABOVE, *A Journey Into Higher Dimensions, pub 2022, followed by TRUE COMPASSION, Merging Love Into Oneness, pub 2023, and now comes DUALITY, In Perspective, … all Titles found on Amazon, Gordon Corwin II.* Other unpublished channel works include those from Ascended Masters Quan Yin and El Morya.

Lah Rahn aka Gordon Corwin currently lives in Oceanside, California and is available for private channelings and group events, and interviews as well as public speaking engagements.

Contact:

GordonCorwin24@gmail.com

Lah@SaintGermainChronicles.com

Light of the Soul Foundation

Established 1998

The Light of the Soul Foundation is a Charitable non-profit 501 (c) (3) Philanthropic Organization founded in 1998 by Gordon Corwin, Trustee.

This non-denominational Foundation is dedicated to

The Spiritual Enlightenment of Humanity.

LOSF continues to be harmoniously bonded with

Highland Light Publishers,

sharing this Spiritual mission that includes writing, publishing and distributing Masters' books in addition to delivering live events with wisdom from The Ascended Masters Above.

"Bringing the Light of Spirit into the _every-day lives_ and _consciousness_ of the masses in an increasingly troubled earthly world … is the practical gift We lovingly offer".

As you now may observe, the collective behavior of Humanity present dark and pervasive behaviors that prevail without change. Your kind philanthropy, donations, and bequests provide the financial means enabling Us to continue serving and delivering
Enlightenment from Above,
expanding Our outreach of Light.

Your donations are transformed into the highest vibrations to all Ones aspiring to reach and live their full Dharma's potential of heightened awareness, Love, Compassion and Soul evolvement … which awaits Humanity.

Light of the Soul Foundation

Charitable Non-profit 501 (c) (3)

Public Events and Spiritual Counseling

IRS **EIN: 91-1945098**

For Your Gifts, Donations, or Bequest Confirmations,
By Check, Credit Card or Bank Wire.

We are deeply grateful to Donors, Contributors and
Philanthropists for your fine and generous *Gifts of Grace
to uplift The Human Consciousness.*

You are an
immensely essential resource that ongoingly empowers
Our continuing Outreach.

For two decades, We have delivered gifts of
Soul Enlightenment and Practical Spirituality via
recently published channeled works, along with public events
and Spiritual readings … with your generous support!

Many Thanks and Blessings. *You All* are
Most Appreciated!

Gratefully yours, Gordon Corwin / Lah Rahn

Please Contact: Trustee, Gordon Corwin, Oceanside,
CA 92056

Gordoncorwin24@gmail.com   or
Lah@SaintGermainChronicles.com

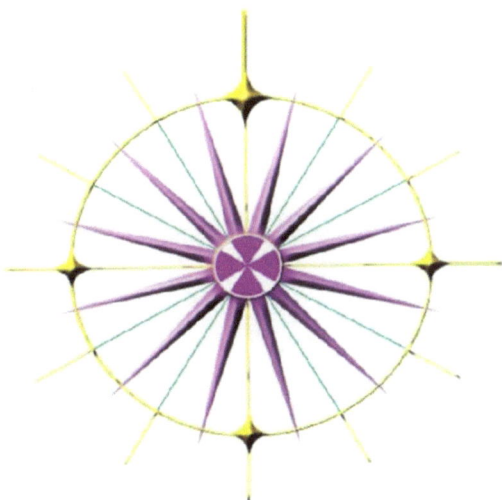

Light of the Soul Foundation

(501)(c)(3)

EIN: 91-1945098

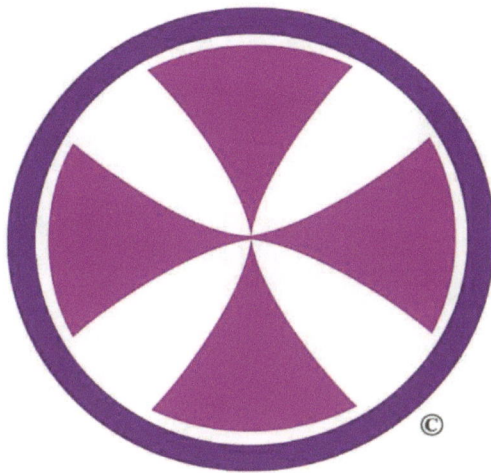

Contact Lah Rahn: Lah@saintgermainchronicles.com

Gordoncorwin24@gmail.com

NOTES

NOTES